TABLE OF CONTENTS

THE SCIENCE OF READING

Reading is an essential skill for success in school and in life. In order to understand how children learn to read, parents should understand the science of reading.

The *science of reading* is a term that refers to more than 20 years of research by experts on how people learn to read. The research shows that reading does not come naturally. For many people, it takes significant effort. Learning how to read is most effective when it happens in a step-by-step process that is based on proven, research-supported strategies and techniques.

Good reading instruction has several important parts. It helps students develop skills in phonological awareness, phonics, fluency, vocabulary, and comprehension. All these skills help students build pathways in their brains that connect speech sounds to print and that connect words with their meanings. By using the science of reading as a guide, parents and teachers can support our children in learning how to read.

KEYS TO EFFECTIVE READING INSTRUCTION

Phonological Awareness: The ability to notice, think about, and work with the sounds that make up spoken words

Phonics: Understanding the relationship between sounds and the letters that represent them in written words

Fluency: The ability to read quickly and accurately

Vocabulary: Understanding word meanings

Comprehension: Gaining meaning from reading

CREATING SKILLED READERS

Reading is more than just sounding out words. Skilled readers are able to recognize words as well as understand their meanings on a deep level. They weave together memorization skills, phonics skills, vocabulary skills, background knowledge, and more.

SCARBOROUGH'S READING ROPE

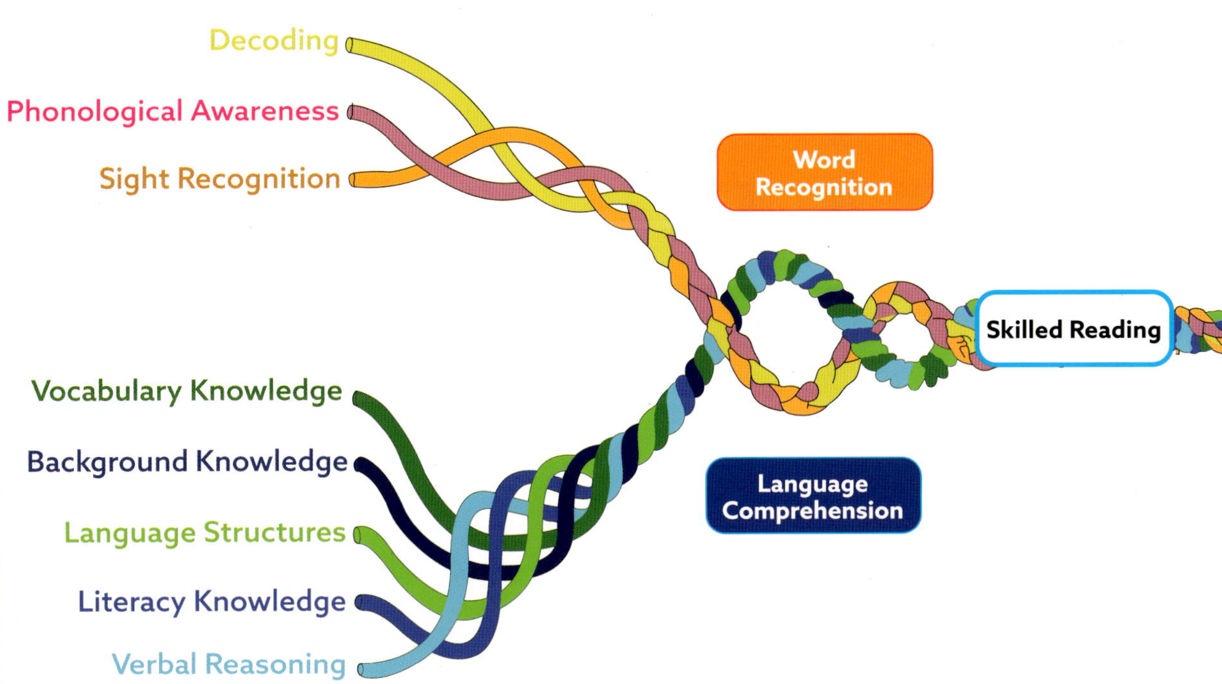

To show how children draw on a variety of abilities to become skilled readers, Dr. Hollis Scarborough created the Reading Rope. In 2001, this model was published in the *Handbook of Early Literacy Research* (Neuman/Dickinson).

WORD ATTACK SKILLS: WORDS HAVE PARTS

Skilled readers can look at unfamiliar words and chunk them, or break them into smaller parts. This helps them attack words and figure out how to read them and what they mean. When readers use chunking, they are sometimes looking at the letters in words. Sometimes, they are looking at the syllables that make up words. Other times, they are looking at prefixes, suffixes, and other word parts. Typically, skilled readers are doing all three. Knowing how to break down words is important for growing as a reader and developing fluency. Fourth graders encounter an increasing number of longer words in their school day. Having good word attack skills is essential.

TYPES OF SYLLABLES

CLOSED	OPEN	MAGIC E	VOWEL TEAM	R-CONTROLLED	CONSONANT + LE
hat rab-bit	me ba-by	time rep-tile	coat rac-coon	farm mar-ket	cas-tle ap-ple
Consonant is after the vowel.	Vowel is at the end of the syllable.	Has the vowel-consonant-silent *e* pattern.	Has two or more vowel letters together.	Vowel is followed by the letter *r*.	Has consonant and *le* at the end of a word.
short vowel sound	long vowel sound	long vowel sound	long, short, or special sound	/ar/, /or/, /ur/	consonant + /l/ sound

BREAKING DOWN A WORD

Compound Word: Is it made of two smaller words? Draw a line between them.

Suffix (Ending): Does it end in *-ed*, *-ing*, *-ful*, *-tion*, etc.? Draw a line before the suffix.

Prefix (Beginning): Does it begin with *pre-*, *un-*, *dis-*, etc.? Draw a line after the prefix.

Double Letters: Do double consonants come between two vowels? Draw a line between the double consonants.

V-C-C-V: Are there two consonants (that don't make one sound together) between two vowels? Draw a line between the two consonants.

V-C-V: Is there one consonant between two vowels? Or a consonant team between two vowels?

-Try drawing a line after the first vowel. That makes the first syllable open and the vowel long. Is that a word? If not, try the first vowel as short *e*. Is that a word?

-Try drawing a line after the consonant or consonant team. That makes the first syllable closed and the vowel short. Is that a word?

ACTIVITIES FOR BUILDING WORD ATTACK SKILLS

CHALLENGE

Get a list of four-, five-, and six-syllable words. Use a timer to see who is the fastest at using their syllable, chunking, and phonics skills to read the words.

Make the Word

Get a list of two-syllable words. Write each syllable on a separate index card. Each word will have one card for the first syllable and one card for the second syllable. Mix up all the cards and place them facedown. The first player flips over two cards. If they make a word, the player keeps the cards and goes again. If the cards do not make a word, the player flips them back over and the next player tries to make a match. Keep going until all cards have a match. The person with the most words wins.

SYLLABLE HUNT

Choose one type of syllable (for example, closed syllables) or one strategy for breaking down a word (for example, dividing between double consonants). Search in books for words that have that type of syllable or that work with that dividing strategy. Write them in a list. How many can you find?

VIDEO TEACHER

Work with your child to create a short video that teaches others how to use the syllable rules to break large words into parts. With your child's approval, share it with your child's teacher.

FLUENCY: READING WITH EASE

Fluency is the ability to read with reasonable speed and expression. A fluent reader doesn't have to stop to decode each word. They can focus on what the story or text means. Fluency is the bridge between decoding words and comprehension.

Your fourth grader is reading smoothly. When they read aloud, their tone and expression change to match the meaning of the text and to respond to what is happening in the story. Most fourth graders begin the school year reading about 90 to 100 words per minute. The goal is to read 120 to 140 words per minute by the end of the year. The best way to increase this speed is to practice, practice, practice.

RECORD IT

After your child practices reading a book, make an audio or video recording of them reading the book aloud. Play it back. Discuss what went well and what to improve on. If your child desires, record again.

FINDING BOOKS THAT ARE JUST RIGHT

ACTIVITIES FOR BUILDING FLUENCY

BOOK OF THE WEEK CHALLENGE

Choose a reading selection that has about 75 to 100 words. On Sunday, read it together at least once. Set a timer and have your child read it aloud. Record the time it takes your child to read. Note if your child needed help. Read the same selection on Monday. Time your child again and note if help was needed. Continue the process every day for a week. At the end, show your child the evidence of how they are improving in fluency.

TRACK IT

Select a chapter book page or another reading selection that has at least 100 words. Use the "Just Right" guidelines below to make sure the reading level of the page is right for your child. Create a fluency tracker chart like the one shown at right. Label it with the name of the reading selection. Set a timer for 60 seconds. Have your child begin reading. Remind them to focus on reading with expression, not just on speed. When the timer goes off, mark the fluency tracker. At the bottom of one column, note the date and the number of words read correctly in one minute. Shade the column to show how many words were read. Use a different color for each day your child practices.

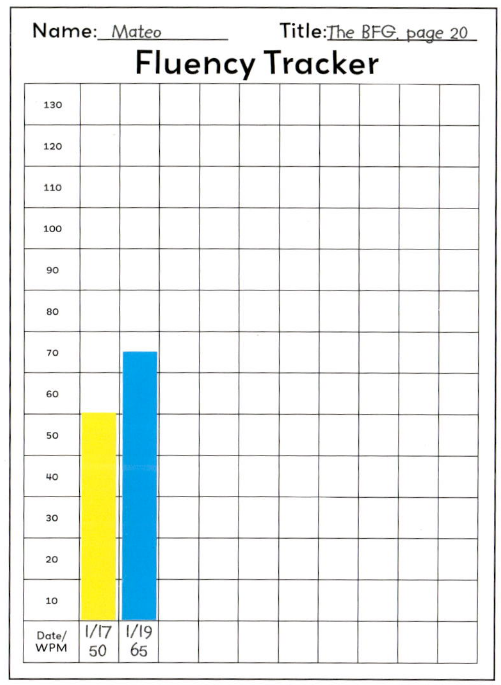

TOO EASY

- You know all the words.
- You can easily retell the story.
- You have read the book many times before.
- You are reading too fast.

Does this describe your book? Try a more difficult book.

JUST RIGHT

- You know most of the words.
- You understand what you are reading, and you can retell it.
- You are reading at a steady pace.

Does this describe your book? This book is just right for you!

TOO HARD

- There are lots of tricky words.
- You forget important information as you read.
- You are reading too slowly.

Does this describe your book? Try an easier book.

VOCABULARY:
WORDS HAVE MEANING

Vocabulary plays a critical role in the process of reading. In order to understand what they read, children must know what the words mean. They need a large mental "word bank" to draw on as they read. This includes two important types of vocabulary: expressive vocabulary, which is used to communicate ideas, and receptive vocabulary, which is used to receive and understand information through reading and listening.

It is important to look at vocabulary from multiple angles. Children will be most successful when their vocabularies have both breadth and depth. That is, they need to know lots of words as well as have a rich understanding of what words mean. Having good vocabulary skills lets children choose the precise word to capture a thought. It lets them connect and categorize words to build a strong knowledge base.

MAP IT!

Create a thinking map. Write a vocabulary word in the center of a sheet of paper. Then, divide the paper into four sections. In the first box, write a simple definition. In the second box, write examples or words that mean the same as the vocabulary word. In the third box, make a connection to something in your life or something you know. In the fourth box, add a picture that represents the word.

Definition	Examples/Synonyms
absolutely necessary or extremely important	water air needed
Connection	**Picture**
It is essential that I drink water.	

essential

TYPES OF VOCABULARY

Listening Vocabulary: The words we hear

Speaking Vocabulary: The words we say

Reading Vocabulary: The words we read

Writing Vocabulary: The words we use to write

ACTIVITIES FOR BUILDING VOCABULARY

WORDS FROM NONFICTION

When your child reads a nonfiction book or article, talk about the new words they learned that relate to the topic. Have your child share with others the new words they learned.

NEW WORD SHARE

Every day, have one family member teach the whole family a new word. Together, create a poster, song, or skit that includes the word's definition, similar words, a sentence that uses the word, and a drawing. Look for opportunities to use the new words in conversation.

NEW WORDS WHILE READING

When your child is reading, it is okay to stop to discuss a new word. Reread the sentence and ask what your child thinks the new word means. Give a child-friendly definition. Help your child make a personal connection to the word.

MY VOCABULARY JOURNAL

Have your child keep a vocabulary journal. Use a spiral-bound notebook or composition book. Write one vocabulary word on each page. Draw a picture that represents the word. Include a definition and a sentence that uses the word. Keep separate notebooks for math, science, social studies, and language arts.

VOCABULARY:
THE POWER OF BASE WORDS, PREFIXES, AND SUFFIXES

Many words in the English language are closely related. It is possible to create new words by adding different beginning and ending parts to base words. Think of the base word *connect*. It can stand alone, but its meaning changes when prefixes and suffixes are added to build words such as *disconnect* and *connectivity*.

Word roots are like base words, except that they cannot stand alone. They need another part to become a word. More than half of English words come from Greek or Latin roots. Fourth graders are beginning to read more technical books and articles. Word roots can help them read and understand about 75 percent of the vocabulary words found in these texts. Learning a few roots, prefixes, and suffixes can help children determine the meaning of many new words. This allows them to comprehend more challenging reading material.

COMMON WORD PARTS AND MEANINGS

Word Roots

aqua: water (aquarium)
aud: to hear or listen (audio)
auto: self (automobile)
bio: life (biology)
cent: one hundred (percent)
fac: to do, to make (factory)
graph: to write (autograph)
hydr: water (hydration)
magni: big or great (magnify)
meter: to measure (thermometer)
multi: many (multiple)
port: to carry (transport)
struct: to build (construct)
therm: heat (thermometer)
vis: to see (invisible)

Prefixes

de: off, opposite (defrost)
dis: not, opposite (disagree)
fore: before, in front (forearm)
in/im: not (indirect, imbalance)
mid: middle (midfield)
non: not (nonsense)
re: again (redo)
sub: under (subway)
un: not, opposite (unusual)

Suffixes

able/ible: is, can be (affordable, sensible)
er/or: person who (gardener, professor)
er: more (taller)
est: the most (tallest)
ful: full of (helpful)
ize: become (civilize)
less: without (hopeless)
ment: state of being (contentment)
y: characterized by (smelly)

ACTIVITIES FOR BUILDING VOCABULARY SKILLS

SING IT

Write a song about words that share roots, prefixes, or suffixes. Create visuals, such as signs or hand gestures, to help teach the meaning of the word part. Perform the song and make a video to share.

MAP IT

Draw a circle in the middle of a sheet of paper. Inside, write a root, prefix, or suffix. Add the meaning of the word part. Then, think of four words that use the root, prefix, or suffix. In each corner of the page, write a different word. Add an illustration and a sentence that uses the word.

Word: *exhale*
Sentence: *Exhale as you bend forward.*
Illustration:

Word: *excavate*
Sentence: *They will excavate this area for the basement.*
Illustration:

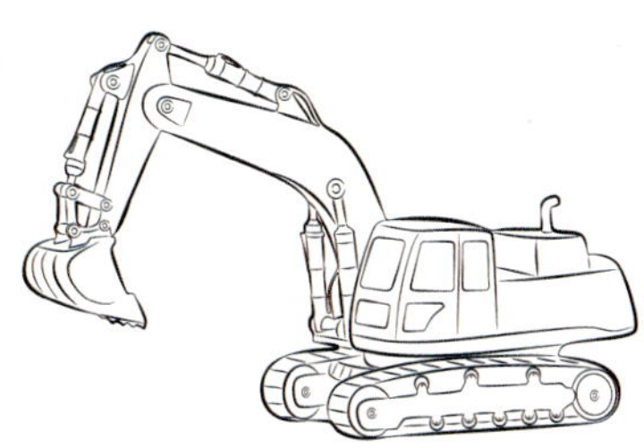

Prefix: *ex-*
Meaning: *out of*

Word: *exchange*
Sentence: *We exchange gifts every year.*
Illustration:

Word: *exclaimed*
Sentence: *She exclaimed in joy when she saw the surprise.*
Illustration:

COMPREHENSION:
UNDERSTANDING
WHAT IS READ

Reading comprehension is the essence of reading. It is the ability to gain meaning from what you read. This is a complex skill that develops over time. For deep comprehension, children's minds must be "turned on" and thinking actively about what they are reading.

Fourth graders are fluent readers. They can go beyond simple comprehension of story plots and facts and analyze the books they read by grasping complex concepts. They can think deeply about how the morals and messages in stories relate to their own lives. They compare and contrast texts. They are aware of how texts are organized and can use text features such as headings and captions to gain additional meaning. Fourth graders can put clues together to make inferences about what they read.

LOL!	Funny part
*	Important part
!	Exciting part or amazing fact
?	Confusing part or unknown word
	Part where I made a connection
+/−	Part I agree with or disagree with
E	Part that contains evidence
	Part where I made an inference

ACTIVE READING WITH SNOTS

Active reading happens when the reader is involved and engaged with the text. The reader is thinking about what is being read and making connections.

Have your child write Small Notes On The Side (SNOTS) to practice active reading and show their thinking. They can draw the symbols shown above on sticky notes to put in the text.

ACTIVITIES FOR BUILDING READING COMPREHENSION

SHARED READING

Choose a book. Read aloud the first paragraph or first couple of sentences. Talk about what was read. Have your child read the next paragraph or couple of sentences. Continue to discuss the text as you share the reading.

CONNECT IT

Help your child make connections to what they are reading. Ask these questions.

Text-to-Self: How does the story or text connect to your life?

Text-to-Text: How does the story or text connect to something else you have read?

Text-to-World: How does the story or text connect to an event, an issue, or something else in the larger world?

READING IS THINKING

QUESTION:
Ask questions before, during, and after reading.

CONNECT:
Connect the text to what you know and who you are.

PREDICT:
Use text clues to infer what will happen next.

VISUALIZE:
Make a movie in your mind while you read.

SUMMARIZE:
Focus on the key ideas.

INFER:
Combine your background knowledge with text clues to make inferences.

SYNTHESIZE:
Make new meaning as you read.

COMPREHENSION: UNDERSTANDING LITERARY TEXTS

Literary texts tell a story. They include novels, short stories, poetry, and drama. Reading literature helps children use their imaginations. As they read about the thoughts and experiences of different characters, children develop empathy for other people.

All literary texts are organized around elements of fiction such as character, setting, plot events, and theme. These elements encourage children to think about cause and effect as they consider how characters respond to circumstances and make choices. Reading literature exposes your child to rich models of language. As they read stories, they learn new words and sentence patterns.

ELEMENTS OF FICTION

All stories have these elements in common.

ACTIVITIES FOR BUILDING READING COMPREHENSION

MY FAVORITE BOOK

Do you have a favorite storybook or chapter book from childhood? Share it with your child. Find a comfy place to take turns reading together out loud. Stop to discuss characters and events as you read. Then, go to the library, bookstore, or online to discover new favorites to read together.

BE AN INFERENCE DETECTIVE!

Sometimes, information is not directly stated. Instead, the reader must use their own knowledge along with clues from the text to draw a conclusion by making an inference. For example, if a person comes in from outside holding a wet umbrella, you can infer that it is raining outside. Making inferences is like being a detective. It takes time and practice. Follow these steps.

Step 1: Ask questions.

Step 2: Find evidence that could answer the questions.

Step 3: Make a conclusion based upon reasoning and evidence.

COMPREHENSION QUESTIONS FOR LITERARY TEXTS

Key Ideas and Details

- Why does this event happen? How do you know?
- How do the main character's actions change what happens in the story?
- What big problem does the main character have? How does the problem get solved?
- What are the main character's personality traits?
- What is the lesson or moral of the story?
- Why did the author write this? What evidence supports your idea?

Craft and Structure

- What does this word or phrase mean? How do you know?
- How are the parts of the story connected?
- Who is telling the story? How do you know?
- Are the narrator and the author the same person? How do you know?
- How would you retell this story?

Integration of Ideas and Knowledge

- What does this illustration show?
- How is the movie version the same? Different?
- For books in a series, what stays the same from story to story? What changes?

COMPREHENSION: UNDERSTANDING INFORMATIONAL TEXTS

Informational texts provide facts and explain ideas. Their purpose is to inform the reader about a specific topic. They include articles, science and history books, autobiographies, and instruction manuals. As they read informational texts, children build background knowledge and learn about the larger world.

Part of comprehending informational texts is learning how they are organized and how to use their features. Recognizing organizational patterns such as compare-and-contrast and problem-solution helps students make sense of complex information. Learning to find and use text features such as headings, captions, and glossaries helps readers navigate, make connections, and understand.

TEXT STRUCTURE TYPES	Definition	Key Words	Graphic Organizer
Compare and Contrast	The author shows how two or more things are alike and different.	similar, alike, different than, both, on the other hand	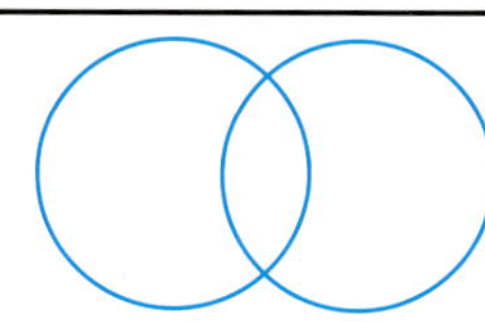
Sequence	The author presents events in time order or in step-by-step order.	first, second, third, after that, then, finally, lastly	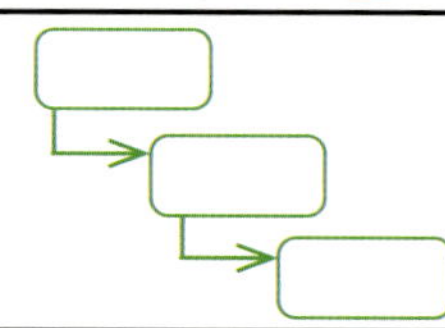
Cause and Effect	The author describes what happens as a result of an event or a decision.	if, then, because, due to, as a result, since	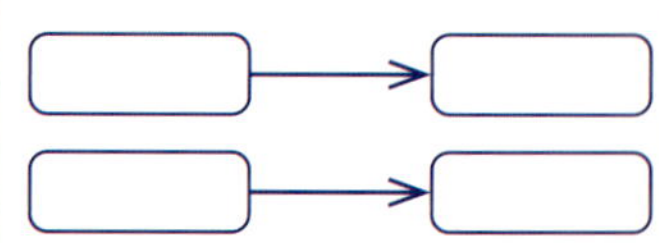
Description	The author describes in detail the parts of something or the characteristics of something.	left, right, top, bottom, for example, for instance, specifically	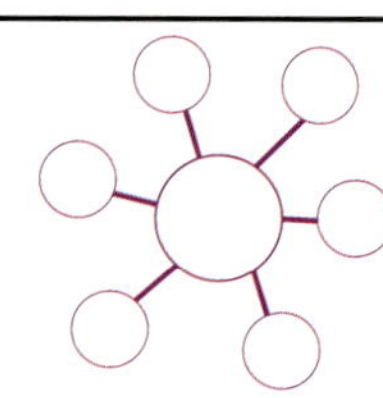
Problem-Solution	The author shows a problem and explains at least one solution.	so, because of, solve, issue, due to, lead to a problem	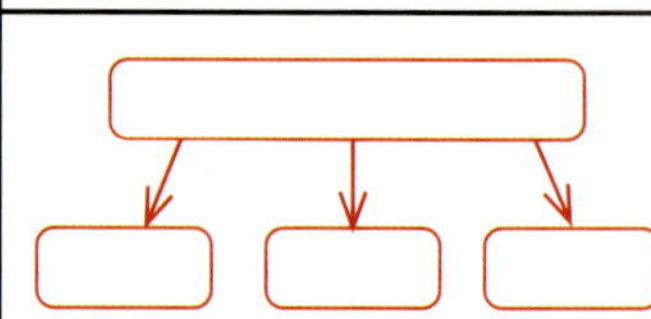

ACTIVITIES FOR BUILDING READING COMPREHENSION

READ AND RESEARCH TOGETHER

Choose a topic that you and your child would like to learn more about. Fold a sheet of notebook paper in half vertically. On the left side, have your child write three to five questions about the topic. Then, research the topic using books and trustworthy websites. On the right side of the paper, your child can write an answer for each question.

TEXT FEATURE SCAVENGER HUNT

When reading informational books, challenge your child to find each text feature. Talk about how the feature helps the reader navigate and understand the information.

Print Features

- ✔ Table of Contents
- ✔ Glossary
- ✔ Index

Graphic Aids

- ✔ Illustrations
- ✔ Diagrams
- ✔ Graphs, Charts, Tables
- ✔ Maps
- ✔ Timelines

Organizational Aids

- ✔ Words in Bold or Italics
- ✔ Titles
- ✔ Headings and Subheadings
- ✔ Sidebars

COMPREHENSION QUESTIONS FOR INFORMATIONAL TEXTS

Key Ideas and Details

- What evidence can you find to show ___?
- What is the main idea? What details tell more about the main idea?
- What do you think the author wants readers to know?
- What are the most important events/ideas/steps to remember? Why?
- How does ____ lead to ___?
- What causes _____? What effect does it have?

Craft and Structure

- What does this word mean? How did you figure out the meaning?
- What is the structure of the text (compare and contrast, cause and effect, etc.)?
- In what other way could the author have organized the information?
- Why did the author write this?
- Do you agree with the author? Why or why not?

Integration of Ideas and Knowledge

- What does this illustration or diagram show? Can you explain it?
- What does the author claim? What evidence supports the claim?
- How is this text like another text you have read?

WRITING: SHOWING UNDERSTANDING

Children are often asked to write about what they read. They also write about their own ideas. When children write, they show their comprehension, vocabulary knowledge, and more. They demonstrate that they have internalized what they have learned and made it their own.

Fourth grade students are writing with clarity and structure. They use transition words such as *because* and *however*. Their sentences are longer and more meaningful. Spelling is more accurate. Punctuation is used appropriately. There is correct subject-verb agreement.

WHEN WRITING IS HARD

- Use a text-to-speech feature on a computer. Then, have your child copy on paper.
- Use a thinking map. Write the topic in a box at the top of a sheet of paper. Underneath, draw three smaller boxes. Write or draw one detail or example in each small box. Use the map to help write a paragraph.
- Have your child tell you what to write. Help them create the sentences. When you are finished, your child can copy what you wrote.
- When your child starts writing, set a timer for 10 minutes. When the timer goes off, take a 10-minute break. Continue this pattern until the writing is complete.

ACTIVITIES FOR BUILDING WRITING SKILLS

POPPING WORDS

Good, big, nice. Some words are generic and don't make writing come alive. In a journal, write a generic word at the top of a page. Below, write more descriptive words that could replace it. As you find more words that add "pop" to your writing, add them to the journal. Use these examples.

good: *excellent, delightful, amazing*

big: *huge, gigantic, enormous*

nice: *kind, thoughtful, gracious*

COMBINE SENTENCES

Encourage your child to write longer, more complex sentences by combining two shorter sentences. Make it a game. Give each other pairs of short sentences to put together into one longer sentence. Can even more information be added to each longer sentence? Use these examples.

The corn was tasty.
The beans were tasty.
The corn and beans were tasty.

It was a nice day.
We had a picnic.
It was a nice day, so we had a picnic.

KEEP A JOURNAL

Encourage your child to keep a writing journal. It can include diary entries, questions, drawings, ideas, and lists. Occasionally, provide prompts for journal entries. For example, say, "Write about what you would like to do this summer" or "Write something you wonder about."

EDITING CHECKLIST

Read aloud. Does it make sense?

- ✔ Are there any words missing?
- ✔ Do all subjects and verbs agree?
- ✔ Is punctuation used correctly in each sentence?
- ✔ Are capital letters used at the beginning of sentences and proper names?
- ✔ Are all words spelled correctly?

WRITING:
HAVING A PURPOSE

Fourth graders write for a variety of purposes. They write to provide information, give opinions, and tell stories. They can write multi-paragraph essays that refer to research sources and that use reasons, facts, and details to strengthen arguments. Planners and graphic organizers help student writers structure their thoughts.

Fourth grade students can write well-developed essays that include an introduction with a main idea, paragraphs that provide details, examples, and reasons to support the main idea, and a closing paragraph that restates the main idea. Using rubrics can help students evaluate their writing and decide what can be improved.

TYPES OF WRITING

Narrative Writing: Tells a story

Informative Writing: Gives information

Opinion Writing: Gives an opinion

INFORMATIVE/OPINION WRITING RUBRIC

Help your child use a rubric to understand expectations for their writing. Read and review this sample rubric with your child.

	4 ★★★★	3 ★★★	2 ★★	1 ★
Main Idea	The main idea is clearly stated.	The main idea is mostly clear.	The main idea is somewhat clear.	The main idea is unclear.
Organization	The essay is well organized.	The essay is mostly well organized.	The essay is somewhat organized.	The essay is disorganized.
Evidence	At least three pieces of evidence support the main idea.	At least two pieces of evidence support the main idea.	At least one piece of evidence supports the main idea.	The main idea is not supported by evidence.
Conventions	Grammar, spelling, and punctuation are at least 90% correct.	Grammar, spelling, and punctuation are at least 75% correct.	Grammar, spelling, and punctuation are at least 50% correct.	Grammar, spelling, and punctuation are less than 50% correct.

ACTIVITIES FOR BUILDING WRITING SKILLS

DETAILS, PLEASE

Choose a nonfiction book. Write the book's topic in the center of a sheet of paper and circle it. As your child reads, they can write details inside more circles that surround the center circle. Draw a line to connect each detail circle to the topic circle. Once there are at least four details, write a paragraph about the topic.

FAMILY STORIES

Encourage your child to learn your family's history by talking to you and to other relatives about stories from the past. What sport did Grandpa play when he was young? What happened to Aunt Rose on a camping trip? Your child can listen to lots of stories and then choose a favorite to write and illustrate. Publish the story by sharing it with family members.

PLAN AN INFORMATIVE ESSAY

Help your child fill in a planner like the one shown here to organize ideas for a well-developed essay that provides information.

Paragraph 1:
Introduction with Main Idea ____________

Paragraphs 2 to 4:
Topic/Main Idea Sentence ____________
Supporting Detail #1 ____________
Supporting Detail #2 ____________
Supporting Detail #3 ____________
Closing Sentence ____________

Paragraph 5:
Conclusion ____________

PLAN AN OPINION ESSAY

Help your child fill in a planner like the one shown here to organize ideas for a well-developed essay that states a persuasive opinion or makes a strong argument.

Topic: ____________

Introduction with My Opinion: ____________

Reason #1 with Supporting Evidence: ____________

Reason #2 with Supporting Evidence: ____________

Reason #3 with Supporting Evidence: ____________

Conclusion with Restatement of My Opinion: ____________

STUDY SKILLS:
ORGANIZATION AND SCHEDULING

Fourth graders are beginning to spend more time on homework. That means your child must fit homework time into days that are probably already busy for them and for you. In late elementary school, many students are juggling schoolwork, sports and extracurriculars, playtime, chores, and family time. They need to learn strategies for keeping all these activities in a healthy balance.

You can help by working with your child to set schedules and organize materials. Find out what works for your child. Some students need frequent breaks. Many find success doing homework right after school when their energy levels are still high. All students need a good study space and handy supplies. Whatever you decide, consistency is key. Your child will quickly learn what is expected when the homework schedule and setup is the same from day to day.

BACKPACK ORGANIZATION

An organized backpack saves time and helps your child be prepared. Set aside time every week to clean out and reorganize with your child.

1. Start with a clean and empty backpack.
2. Keep loose supplies in cases.
3. Assign a place for each item, and make sure everything gets returned to its spot.
4. Create a school-to-home folder for flyers and graded work. Have your child place items from this folder into a special bin at home and then immediately put the emptied folder back into the backpack.
5. Create a homework folder that is a different color than the school-to-home folder.
6. Use the agenda or planner that is provided or recommended by your child's school.
7. Ask for extra textbooks to keep at home if online versions are not available.

HOW MUCH TIME?

Your child's teacher can tell you how much time students are expected to spend each day on homework. Typically, students are assigned about 10 to 15 minutes of homework per school grade. That means a fourth grader can expect to spend 40 to 60 minutes each day completing homework.

ACTIVITIES FOR BUILDING STUDY SKILLS

SET UP A STUDY SPACE

Having a study space is important for school success. It should support your child in the way they learn best. Some students need a chair with a back, but others work better standing. Some children like to use a desk or table. Others are more successful working on the floor. Your child may need absolute quiet, or they may benefit from listening to music. All study spaces need supplies, including sharpened pencils and paper, kept very close by.

ESTABLISH ROUTINES

Routines help your child practice good habits. Checklists that you and your child create together are helpful reminders. Post them in easy-to-find areas around the house. Use these samples as a guide.

School Morning Routine

- ✔ Get dressed.
- ✔ Make your bed.
- ✔ Wash your face.
- ✔ Eat breakfast.
- ✔ Brush your teeth.
- ✔ Check to make sure your backpack has what you need for the day.

After-School Routine

- ✔ Empty your school-to-home folder.
- ✔ Eat a snack.
- ✔ Do homework.
- ✔ Set the dinner table.
- ✔ Read for 30 minutes.
- ✔ Practice multiplication facts.

STUDY SKILLS: TAKING NOTES

Writing down important information gives children an opportunity to be active learners. Taking notes fosters concentration and comprehension. When children decide what information is most important to write in a note, they are processing and learning the material. As they use a pencil to write notes by hand, the brain stores the information in memory.

When they first begin to take notes, children will copy word-for-word from the book or from the teacher. Condensing, summarizing, and putting ideas into their own words are skills that take practice and encouragement. There are numerous ways to take notes. Giving your child a variety of note-taking strategies allows them to find the one that works best for what they are learning.

TWO-COLUMN NOTES

One of the easiest methods for taking notes is to make a chart with two columns on a sheet of paper. Label the left side *Topic*. Label the right side *Details*. As your child reads nonfiction books and articles, have them figure out the main topic of each paragraph or section and write it on the left. Then, on the right, they can add two or three details from the paragraph or section.

Another way to use this strategy is to label the first column *My Questions* and the second column *Answers*. Your child can create questions before and during reading. They can write the answers as they discover them in the text.

MEASURING TOOLS

Topic	Details
Ruler	12 inches 1 foot Use for: book, pencil, drawer
Yard Stick	36 inches 3 feet Use for: table, my dog
Measuring tape	60 inches 5 feet Use for: your height, a car

ACTIVITIES FOR BUILDING STUDY SKILLS

CHECK AND CORRECT

Studying from incorrect notes leads to confusion and disappointment. If your child is relying on their notes, take a minute to read them and make sure they don't contain obvious errors. Encourage your child to demonstrate their understanding by explaining their notes to you.

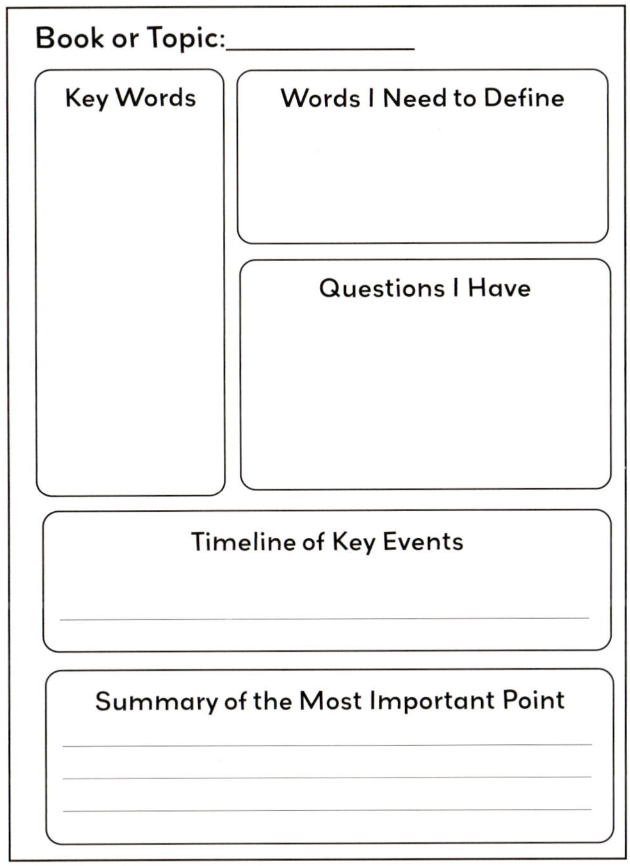

ORGANIZED NOTES

Filling in a planner or graphic organizer can be a great way to help your child think about what they are reading. Use this example.

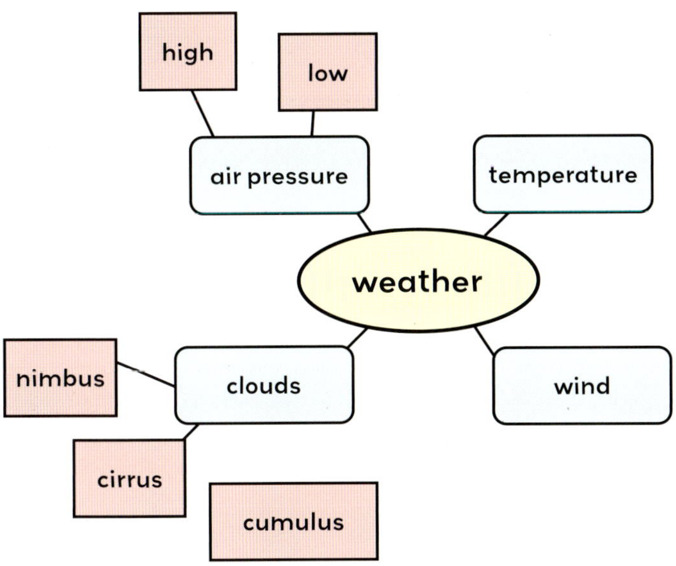

KNOWLEDGE WEBS

Making a web or concept map is another good way to take notes. Write thc main topic inside a center circle. Link more shapes to show subtopics and main ideas. Finally, add shapes for supporting details and examples.

WHAT TO DO WHEN YOUR CHILD STRUGGLES

As a parent, it is frustrating when your child has difficulties. When this happens, it is important to seek out help. Begin with your child's classroom teacher, who might be able to provide more personalized instruction and strategies to try at home. You can also reach out to a reading specialist or special education teacher at your school or district. Tutors, professionals in private practice, and reading clinics are other ways to support your child.

If your child continues to struggle, ask the school to have a meeting that includes the classroom teacher, reading or literacy coach, school psychologist, school counselor, and special education teacher. This is an opportunity for everyone to be honest and open in a supportive way. The goal of such a meeting is to gather information in order to decide how to move forward. Some possible outcomes are formal evaluation for special education, creation of a 504 Plan or Individualized Education Plan (IEP), more intensive instruction by the classroom teacher, or referral to a pediatrician for a possible medical diagnosis.

QUESTIONS FOR TEAM DISCUSSION

- Are there attention issues at school? At home?
- Is poor attendance having an impact?
- When were the child's hearing and vision last checked?
- Does the child speak another language?
- Did the child struggle with reading in previous grades?
- What supports and strategies have been in place? Were they successful?
- Does the child have a medical condition that may impact learning?

HOW TO HELP AT HOME

If your child is reading below grade level, you'll want to enlist the support of their classroom teacher and other experts. However, you have an important role to play. Your encouragement can make a big difference when it comes to your child's attitude about reading, motivation to read, and steady growth as a reader. Try these suggestions.

1. NOTICE STUMBLING BLOCKS

Not all reading problems are alike. You are in a unique position to notice when and why your child is struggling. Read with your child and take note of what is challenging. Then you'll be able to make a plan for getting help. Some reasons for concern are avoidance of reading, slow and labored oral reading, and having trouble with books well below grade level. Share specific observations and concerns with your child's teachers.

2. KEEP READING

Make reading every day a joyful part of your home. Make sure your child has easy access to a variety of reading materials. Let your child see you reading for pleasure and for finding information. Talk about what you are reading and encourage your child to talk about what they are reading. This will lead to rich conversations that help your child build vocabulary and language skills.

3. FIND THE RIGHT BOOKS

Let your child choose books that interest them. Seek out books that relate to your child's interests. Reading books in a series is a good way to encourage reading comprehension as children become familiar with different stories about the same characters. Graphic novels and early chapter books can help children bridge from picture books and read-alouds into more independent reading.

4. HAVE FUN

Sometimes, children get the message that reading is a chore. Make it fun by encouraging your child to draw pictures and write stories about favorite characters, act out stories, and take turns reading aloud with you or with a sibling. By joining in the fun, your child will steadily build skills and grow as a reader.

WORDS TO KNOW

504 Plan: a plan that describes the accommodations that the school will provide to support the student's education

active reading: when a reader is thinking about, involved with, and engaged in a text

decoding: the ability to sound out written words

ELA: English language arts

ELL: English language learner

ESE: exceptional student education

fluency: the ability to read with speed, accuracy, and appropriate expression

high-frequency word: a word that often appears in written material and that can be decoded using common phonics rules

IEP: individualized education plan; a personalized plan that describes the special education instruction, supports, and services a child needs

Lexile level: a scientific measurement of the complexity and readability of a text

literacy: the ability to read and write

phonemic awareness: the ability to identify and manipulate individual sounds in spoken words

phonics: matching the sounds of spoken English to individual letters or groups of letters; the relationship between sounds and letters

phonological awareness: the ability to identify and manipulate syllables and other parts of spoken words

reading comprehension: the ability to understand and interpret what you read

RTI: response to intervention; an educational strategy that aims to identify struggling students early on and give them the support they need to succeed in school

science of reading: a body of research that shows what is most important and effective in reading instruction

sight word: a word that often appears in written material and that can be difficult to decode using common phonics rules

standards: simple statements that describe what students are expected to know or do as a result of what is learned in school

syllable: a word part that contains one vowel sound

Tier 1 instruction: instruction for the whole class that is based on the learning standards for that grade level

Tier 2 instruction: small group instruction for students who demonstrate slight learning challenges in specific areas

Tier 3 instruction: small group instruction for students who need more intensive help and support

vocabulary: knowledge about what words mean

ADDITIONAL INFORMATION

To learn more about the science of reading:
https://teacherblog.evan-moor.com/2022/05/02/what-parents-need-to-know-about-the-science-of-reading/

To learn more about phonological awareness and phonemic awareness:
https://readingteacher.com/what-is-phonological-awareness-and-why-is-it-important/

To learn more about phonics and decoding:
https://www.twinkl.com/teaching-wiki/decoding

To learn more about vocabulary development:
https://www.edutopia.org/article/6-quick-strategies-build-vocabulary/

To learn more about reading comprehension:
https://www.readnaturally.com/research/5-components-of-reading/comprehension

To learn more about IEPs and 504 Plans:
https://www.understood.org/en/articles/the-difference-between-ieps-and-504-plans

Some information for this book came from the following websites:

- Florida Center for Reading Research https://fcrr.org
- Home Reading Helper https://www.homereadinghelper.org
- International Dyslexia Association https://dyslexiaida.org
- North Carolina Department of Public Instruction https://www.dpi.nc.gov
- Reading Rockets https://www.readingrockets.org

Written by: Madison Parker, M.Ed.
Design by: Rhea Magaro-Wallace
Series Development: James Earley
Editor: Kim Thompson

Photo credits: Shutterstock

Library of Congress PCN Data
Helping My Child with Reading Fourth Grade / Madison Parker, M.Ed.
A Guide to Supporting Reading
ISBN 979-8-8904-2115-9 (paperback)
ISBN 979-8-8904-2125-8 (eBook)
ISBN 979-8-8904-2135-7 (ePUB)

Printed in China.

Seahorse Publishing Company
www.seahorsepub.com

Published in the United States
Seahorse Publishing
PO Box 771325
Coral Springs, FL 33077

SEAHORSE PUBLISHING